IS
IT
TRUE ?

Anthony Wootton

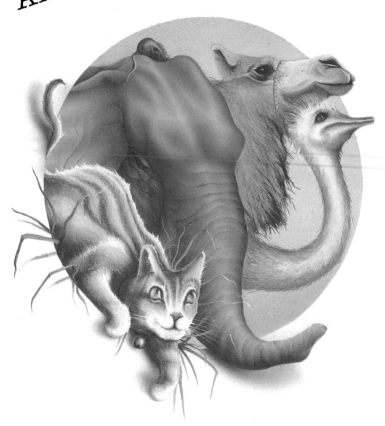

To Sarah, with thanks for being so good about the bull.

CONTENTS

CAN CATS
SEE IN
THE DARK ?

I don't know about you, but I have always admired and even envied cats. They're so independent and take life so easily. What is more, they don't seem to bother about time at all, but give the impression of being equally at home after dark as they are during the day. *We* may fumble about and fall over things without the aid of a light, but a cat appears 'purrfectly' at ease in almost total darkness, leaping over obstacles or hunting for mice, and hardly ever comes to grief. Go into the garden at night to call in your cat for its supper and you may see no more of it than a pair of brilliant yellow-green eyes blazing at you out of the gloom, suggesting that it really can see in the dark with the aid of what look rather like its own built-in headlamps!

Actually, though, appearances are a little deceptive. The plain fact is that no animals — not even wholly nocturnal ones — can see in *total* darkness. There has to be *some* light for animals' eyes to work properly, because they contain a lens, like a telescope or camera, and you wouldn't get much of a picture if you focussed either of these optical instruments on absolute blackness. That is why, if you observe the comings and goings of your cat rather more closely, you'll notice that it prefers to be out of doors (or stays out longer) on moonlit or starlit nights, and is less at ease during evenings when it is overcast with cloud.

Having said that, there is no doubt that cats can see very much better after dark than you and me. In fact, it has been proved that their eyes need only about one-sixth of the light that ours do in order to function properly. To understand why this should be it is probably best to begin by looking at how our own eyes work, and then compare them with the cat's.

As I have said, your eyes each contain a lens, through which the light reflected from whatever you happen to be looking at passes. The image is then focussed on a light-sensitive area at the back of the eye, called the *retina*, which contains special nerve receptors that pass on the image 'message' to the brain. Your eye is very like a camera, not only because it uses a *lens* but because it also contains a special device for controlling the amount of light coming into it. Look at a friend's eyes in different lights and you'll notice that, if the surroundings are bright and well-lit, his *pupils* (that's the central part) are small. This prevents the eye from being blinded by too much light. In the same way, his pupils will be opened to their fullest round extent in the dark, so as to take in as much light as possible. The size of the pupils is altered by special muscles in the immediately surrounding area, called the *iris* (the part which gives your eyes their colour).

The problem with our eyes is that while they perform very well during the day (better than a cat's, in fact!), they are less well adapted for use at night. A cat's eyes are rather different. They are constructed on the same basic principle as ours, of course, but with certain refinements especially designed for night vision.

Firstly, the cat's eye is bigger in relation to the size of the head. This is a help in itself because it means that the brain receives a larger picture of what it sees. Then again, the cat's iris is a different shape from ours, being pointed oval, or elliptical, instead of round. This, too, is useful to the cat because irises of this shape can open up more fully than ours, enabling their owners to take in more light in gloomy conditions; they can also close up to the narrowest of slits, preventing blinding by brilliant sunshine or the sudden glare of a car's headlamps.

Cat's eyes by night...

...and day.

More important still, our cat's eyes possess a special crystal-like layer, called a *tapetum*, behind the retina which is particularly valuable at night because it acts as a reflector and prevents much of the light initially received by the eye from being missed.

The point is, you see, that in our eyes a lot of the light that passes through our lenses after dark is not picked up by the sensitive nerves in the retina but becomes lost and absorbed in the general tissues of the eye. The cat's tapetum, on the other hand, doesn't allow this extra light to be wasted but sends it back to the light-receptors

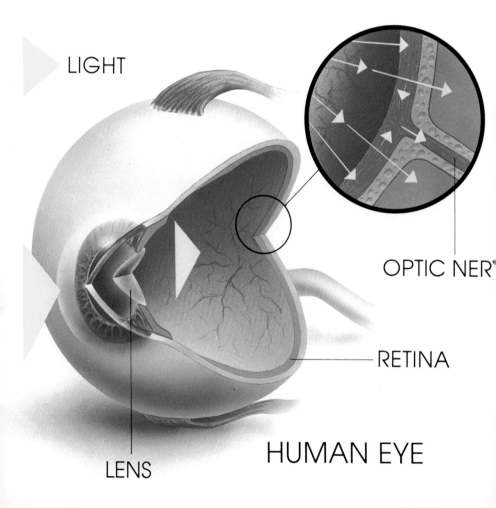

LIGHT

OPTIC NER'

RETINA

LENS

HUMAN EYE

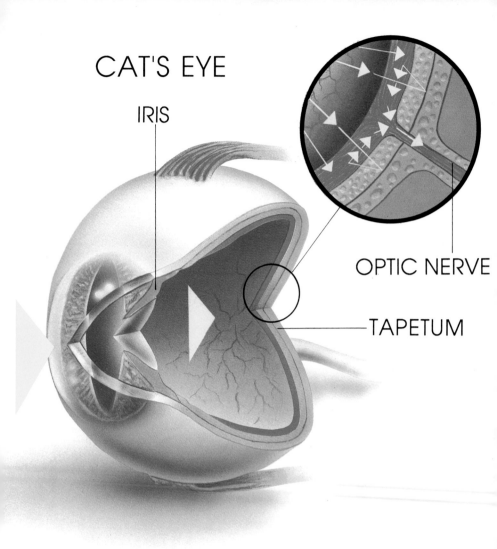

CAT'S EYE

IRIS

OPTIC NERVE

TAPETUM

again. As a result, our cat has, if you like, two chances to see what it is looking at, and so sees things more clearly in dim light than we do. All the cat is really doing, in fact, is making better use of the available light than our day-adapted eyes are able to do.

If you think about it, you'll realise that it is the tapetum layer that makes a cat's eyes seem to glow like live coals. Those 'cat's eyes' set into the middle of roads to help night-drivers are built on exactly the same reflective principle. Invented by a certain Mr Percy Shaw in the 1930's, they proved particularly useful during the 'black-out' days of World War Two (1939-45) because, while visible to drivers, they couldn't be seen by enemy bombers flying overhead.

Now, I wonder where Shaw got his idea from!

THE CATSEYE

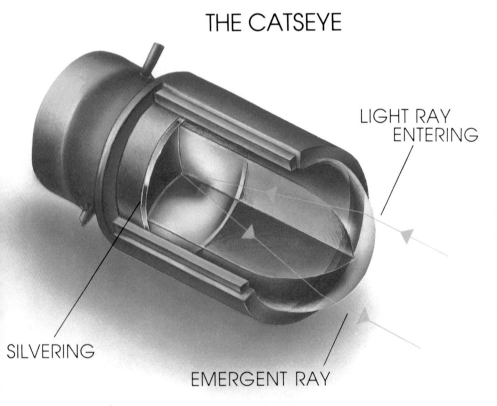

LIGHT RAY ENTERING

SILVERING

EMERGENT RAY

Catseyes in the road have a light-reflecting layer of silvering behind the lens. This acts in the same way as the 'tapetum' which makes a cat's eyes seem to glow in the dark.

DO BULLS

SEE RED ?

Because we humans think and react in certain ways, it is
easy to fall into the trap of believing that animals do
likewise. One example lies in the way we actually see and
look at things. *We* are able to appreciate the beauty of
the world in all its many colours, so we automatically
assume that animals are able to do the same. We even
tend to 'make' animals respond to colours in a human
way. For example, if you 'see red' you suddenly flare up
and lose your temper, just as a red rag is liable (or so it is
thought) to turn a previously placid bull into a snorting,
raging beast. Even today, Spanish bull-fighters wear a
red cape and wave it in front of a bull, following the
tradition that red is the colour to make them suitably
fierce opponents (although the odds are stacked against
the poor animal from the start). Equally, we are told, it
is unwise to go anywhere near a bull in a field if you
happen to be wearing anything red.

The truth is, though, that there is no evidence that bulls take any more notice of red than they do of other colours. We can never be absolutely sure about animal vision, of course, because we cannot actually see through their eyes. But behavioural experiments suggest that bulls and many other mammals have very little perception of colours at all, even though their eyes are constructed in much the same way as ours. They may even be like us in having special structures in their eyes called *cones*, which are directly concerned with distinguishing colours. Unfortunately, many animals, like cattle, either lack some of these cones or they do not function properly. As a result, they have a much more limited idea of colours than we do and may even see things only in black and white or in varying shades of grey. Quite probably, many colours only appear different to animals like these because of the varying amounts of light they reflect, making them lighter or darker, according to intensity. Orange would appear different from brown, for example, as light or darker greys.

The interesting thing is that bulls and many other mammals may be colour-blind in much the same way that some people are, in that they are unable to distinguish red from green — which is, in fact, the most common form of human colour-blindness.

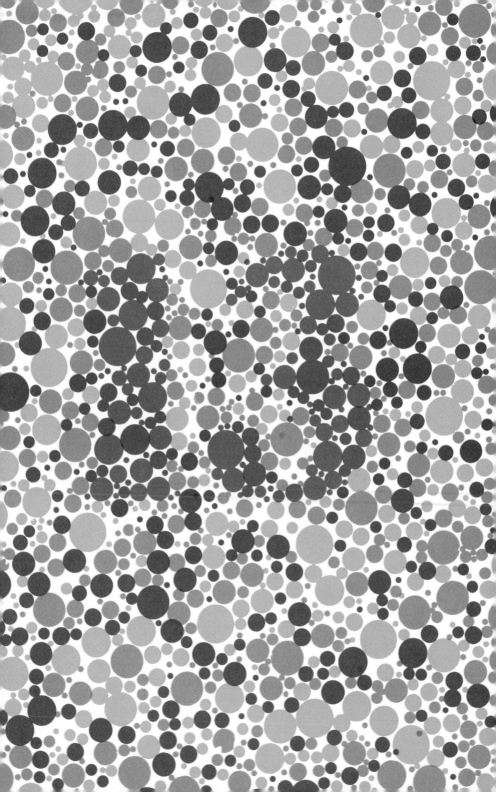

All things considered, then, if a bull does seem to react to something coloured red, it is unlikely to be the colour itself that sets it off. It may be doing so simply out of natural aggression, such as is shown by many male animals. If a bull chased you across a field, it would mean it was protecting its territory and driving off an intruder (you), as well as protecting its cows. Whether you were wearing red, blue or purple with yellow spots makes not the slightest difference.

At first sight, the bull's inability to recognize colours seems rather strange and difficult to explain, We might even feel a little sorry for him. We need not, though, because animals' vision is directly linked to actual need, and varies widely according to group. If you think about it, colour-blindness is no handicap to cattle because they and their wild relatives are grazing animals, and the most interesting and important things to them are grass and hay. They have no need to bother about a range of colours when their whole world is principally concerned with green and yellow or pale brown! In other animals, the need to distinguish colours is greater. Birds, for example, have excellent colour vision because their flight commonly takes them over a wide area and they need to be able to recognize different kinds of foods, such as berries and insects.

Just why we should automatically think of red as being the colour of anger is an interesting point in itself. Perhaps it is because red is the colour of blood, wounds and fire that history has always linked it with aggression, war and general unrest. Red is also, of course, the colour we use for danger warning signs, while political parties and other groups advocating change, tend to choose red, for their symbolic colour. I think most would agree that red is not the most restful colour to have displayed in large areas. Few would choose it for their wallpaper, for example, though I suppose you might be happy with it if

you happened to be a supporter of Liverpool or
Manchester United Football Clubs. Personally, I prefer
the altogether much more soothing green which,
curiously enough, is the colour of *my* local football team!

DO BATS GET IN YOUR HAIR ?

When we watch certain animals going about their
business, it is perhaps not difficult to understand why
our less-knowledgeable ancestors often imagined all sorts
of strange things about them. Nocturnal animals, such
as bats, tended to be particularly misunderstood, and not
just because it was difficult to see exactly what they were

18

up to. Darkness itself was something to be feared, so that any creatures active at night must surely be up to no good, the companions, perhaps, of goblins and evil spirits and other creatures of the devil.

Even today, when we know so much more about them, bats have a certain air of mystery which sets them apart from other animals. Flying after dark in complete silence, apart from an occasional mouse-like squeak, they seem just to appear and disappear at will. Bats are rarely seen during the daytime, but if you do happen to come across them roosting, perhaps in a hollow tree, they look a little like mice with wings. In fact, one old name for the bat was 'flittermouse', suggesting that our forbears felt these little animals might be some sort of strange member of the mouse family.

Australian flying foxes, or fruit bats.

These things, taken together, go some way towards explaining why people in olden times often tended to view bats with deep suspicion. Centuries ago, when people firmly believed in black magic and sorcery, bats were considered to be the natural companions of witches. In fact, many a poor old woman might have been regarded as a witch simply because she happened to have bats roosting in the roof of her cottage. In medieval times, the devil himself was commonly depicted as wearing bat's wings, while no story of Dracula and vampires is complete without bats flitting mysteriously about the castle walls or accompanying human vampires in their bloodsucking activities.

A medieval devil with bat's wings.

Of course, the truth about bats is very different indeed. The only mammals to be able to fly, they are quite unrelated to mice (which are rodents, or gnawing animals), and belong to a separate order of mammals called the *Chiroptera:* a scientific name which comes from two Greek words meaning 'hand-wing', because the bat's wings are constructed on a sort of framework formed by the animal's forearm and elongated fingers. Vampire bats do exist, but they only live in Central and South America and do not occur in Count Dracula's Transylvania or anywhere else in Europe. In any case, vampire bats don't really suck blood at all, but simply make a delicate incision with their sharp teeth and lap up the blood that wells out. They do occasionally take the blood of man but their more usual victims are wild and domestic animals like fowl or cattle. All other bats feed mainly on insects and fruits and are quite harmless to man. Human vampires, needless to say, are complete fiction.

A vampire bat feeds off a live chicken.

It is, however, bats' flight which is, in many ways, the most interesting aspect of their behaviour, if only because it has given rise to a number of largely incorrect beliefs. One of them is comprised in the expression 'blind as a bat', which we commonly use to describe someone who has perhaps mislaid their spectacles or who blunders about in a darkened room and cannot find the light switch. On the face of it, it is difficult to understand why anyone should have ever thought bats blind, because it is clear from their confident, after-dark flight that they know exactly where they are going. In any case, bats have perfectly developed eyes, even if they are generally rather small. However, the old saying is perhaps not quite as stupid as it seems because, at night, bats hardly use their eyes at all but employ a special kind of navigation system which makes vision quite unnecessary.

Bats' method of flying after dark without actually looking where they are going is one of the most remarkable of all natural phenomena. In order to fly with confidence and avoid colliding with obstacles in their path they use a method called echo-location, which involves sending out a stream of electronic pulses from their mouth or nose. The pulses bounce off objects in the bat's line of flight and are returned to the bat, which is able to tell by the time the echoes take to arrive just how far away — and where — the object is.

Bats also use their echo-location system to capture food, which is commonly night-flying insects, such as moths. All this is carried out at lightning speed and is so efficient that the bat rarely makes a mistake. Experiments have been carried out by releasing bats in a room criss-crossed with very fine threads, but the bats rarely touched them much less became entangled with them.

It is, of course, on much the same principle as the bats' night-flying technique that RADAR (Radio Detection And Ranging) and SONAR (Sound Navigation And Ranging) are based. Both of these detection devices were invented at the beginning of World War Two, radar being used for determining the position of aerial objects, such as planes, and sonar for assessing the whereabouts and nature of underwater vessels like submarines. We were rather late in getting around to these ideas, however, because bats are believed to have been using their radar as long as 50 million years ago! We were not even first with sonar, since whales and dolphins employ a somewhat similar system.

This radar scanner, at London's Heathrow Airport, covers most of Southern England.

Bats' radar works so well that we ought to be able to dismiss one particular belief about them as absolute nonsense. This suggests that bats have a way of deliberately or accidentally flying into and becoming entangled in the hair. People often tend to be quite nervous if bats happen to be flying anywhere near them, convinced that the inevitable collision is about to occur! Probably, the idea is at least partly based on the false belief I referred to earlier, that bats are blind and so cannot see where they are going. However, there does seem to be a little more to it than that. Indeed, I have talked to people who swear that they have had something of the kind actually happen to them, and I am certainly not going to label them 'story tellers'!

A greater horseshoe bat.

I accept the accounts because the fact is that bats *have* been known to collide with things, if very rarely. Mainly it happens because of an injury to some part of the bat's body. If one of their ears becomes blocked or damaged, for example, this might affect the way they interpret the echoes they receive from their radar pulses. Errors of judgement can also happen if they have suffered some damage to their vocal chords, which give out their 'range-finding' squeaks. In some bats, like the strange horseshoe bats, damage to the nose could have a similar confusing effect, because in this group the pulses are emitted through the nasal folds. Any of these injuries might cause a bat to make a mistake in judging the distance and nature of things it was flying near to. Apart from all this, bats have been known to make mistakes when they are *not* injured. *Daubenton's* or water bats have been seen to collide with anglers' night lines, perhaps because they mistook the ripples caused by the float for an emerging water insect.

All these things suggest how the 'bat-in-the-hair' legend may have come about. As I have said, bats don't collide with people very often. Indeed, it is a rare occurrence. But that, of course, is precisely how legends are made. If such things occurred all the time, they wouldn't be legends but accepted (bat) behaviour!

A fishing bat - a native of Central America.

DO EARWIGS GET IN YOUR EARS ?

You probably know of the ancient legend that earwigs get in your ears, because the idea is surprisingly widespread even today. I first heard of it a long time ago, as a small boy, whilst talking to an old lady neighbour of ours in her garden one day. We happened to be looking at the earwigs nesting in her prize dahlias and chrysanthemums, and discussing the harm they did, when she suddenly began to tell me a truly harrowing tale of a girl she knew who had somehow got earwigs in her ears and went mad as a result. Eventually, it seems, the poor girl died and when she was examined, *post mortem*, they found a teeming nest of earwigs in her brain!

Yes, I know, the whole thing's almost too horrible even to think about, so let me put your mind at rest straight away. It seems likely that 'my' old lady had, long ago, read one of those horror stories with an earwig theme and, as she grew older and more forgetful, turned fiction into fact. Anyway, she was almost certainly mistaken, because it is very doubtful if an earwig could even burrow its way into the inner ear, much less get as far as the brain. For one thing, its jaws are not strong enough to pierce the gristly eardrum, or *tympanum*, that lies at the end of the passage of the outer ear and shuts it off from the more delicate inner ear. Neither would an earwig use its pincers for this purpose. (The earwig's pincers, or forceps, are probably mainly used in defence, although the male also uses his larger, more strongly curved ones for holding the female during mating.)

There *are* records of earwigs and other small insects making their way into the outer passage of the ear, but such intrusions are very rare. When they occur, it is usually when people have been sleeping out of doors, on the ground, and even then it usually happens by chance. You see, earwigs spend most of their life at ground level and rarely fly. They like to lie up in places that are fairly warm, sheltered and slightly moist, such as under loose bark and in hollow canes, as well as deep in the heart of flowers and vegetables. So if a wandering earwig came across an ear, in exactly the right position, it might feel it served its purpose just as well and use it as a temporary shelter, although it would have no more sinister ideas in mind. However, as I have said, the chances of it happening at all are remote. In fact, getting an earwig in your ear is considerably less likely than having a fly land in your eye when you are playing tennis or cricket, so there's no need to let the idea put you off camping!

The interesting thing is that even foreign names for the earwig may have been misunderstood for centuries. The French name for it is *perce-oreille,* which means literally 'ear-piercer', but again it's almost certainly nowhere near as bad as it sounds. Most people say it refers merely to the shape of the male earwig's pincers, or forceps, which are just like the tool once used for piercing the ear-lobes for earring fitting! The French name can be traced back at least to the 16th century and since the French language was for many centuries the standard language of communication throughout much of Europe it seems likely that other European names for the earwig derive from the French. (For example, the Portuguese name for earwig, *fura-orelhas,* also means 'ear-piercer'.) Perhaps that is where the widespread continental mistrust of the earwig comes from, too!

Medieval ear-piercers.

To sum up, then, there is absolutely no reason to be nervous of earwigs, even when they occasionally venture indoors and perhaps get into your clothes, towel, or even your bed, because they have no dark motives in mind when they do. It is just that they like warmth (even being covered up) and are also great scavengers on such tiny food scraps as they can find. They are not, perhaps, the most attractive of insects, yet we ought really to admire them, if only because they are among the few insects to actually care for their young. Most insects, including the handsomest butterflies, just lay their eggs and leave the hatched larvae to fend for themselves, but the female earwig actually broods her eggs, like a hen bird. She also feeds and guards the baby nymphs until they are strong enough to live independently. If her site is disturbed, she may even pick up her youngsters by the scruff of the neck and transfer them to a safer place.

A female earwig with her young.

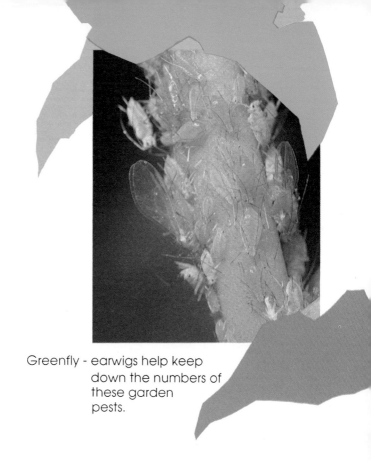

Greenfly - earwigs help keep
down the numbers of
these garden
pests.

The earwig's bad image as a garden pest tends to be exaggerated, too. It does eat some cultivated plants and flowers, but it also commonly consumes waste material as well as a variety of small soft-bodied insects, such as blackfly and greenfly, which really *are* pests.

Like them or loathe them, there seems little doubt that earwigs have long been misunderstood and deserve our better opinion.

DO CROCODILES REALLY CRY ?

It is never wise to judge animals (or people) from their appearance alone, yet that is just what our ancestors often did, especially if the animals concerned were dangerous to approach — like crocodiles. Even today, if you look at a crocodile in a zoo, it is easy to feel that this great reptile is enjoying some sort of private joke, as it lies there with what looks like a fixed grin about its mouth. When it spreads its great jaws wide, it might even be said to be caught in mid-laugh!

Needless to say, the crocodile isn't really amused. It is simply that the structure of its mouth, allowing for the articulation of those huge, impressively toothed jaws makes it *look* as if it is always smiling. The upturned corners of your cat's or dog's mouth present a rather similar appearance.

If you watch a crocodile at feeding time you may notice another aspect of its behaviour which once gave people quite the wrong impression. When the crocodile seizes its food — which, in the wild, is usually living — it often weeps profusely, suggesting that it is really quite sorry for what it is doing. So it was that when people observed these two things about the crocodile — its fixed grin and tears — their immediate feeling was that the reptile was being nothing less than a hypocrite and displaying sorrow it didn't really feel. The idea has, of course, become a part of our everyday language as 'crocodile tears', which we use when someone puts on a show of regret about something but is secretly rather pleased about it, perhaps because he or she is going to benefit in some way or gain from someone else's misfortune.

Once again, of course, the link is quite false, because the crocodile is not really crying — at least, not in the sense that *we* cry. In fact, it is probable that only humans cry when they are sad or happy (remember we

A Nile crocodile - don't trust the smile!

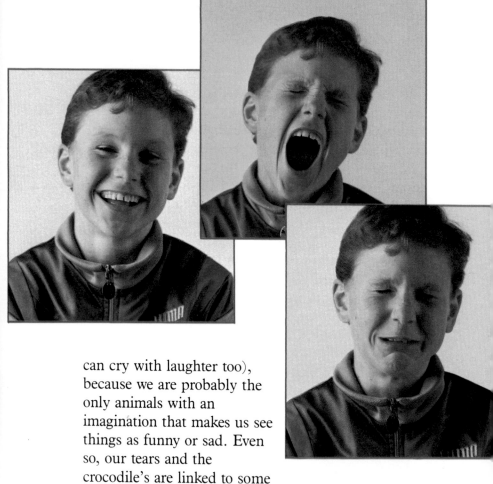

can cry with laughter too), because we are probably the only animals with an imagination that makes us see things as funny or sad. Even so, our tears and the crocodile's are linked to some extent. When the crocodile opens its mouth very widely to take in its prey (which can often be quite large), the jaws exert pressure on special *lachrymal* or tear glands close to the eyes, causing them to 'water'. We have exactly the same glands in our eyes and a rather similar effect to the crocodile's occurs when we yawn widely. Think, too, what happens when you (genuinely) cry: mostly you wrinkle up your face, so that this, too, affects the tear glands.

There are other reasons why animals and people cry, too. In fact, to some extent, we are always crying because every time we blink a little lachrymal fluid is washed over the delicate eyeball to keep it clear of dust particles.

Animals' eyes work in just the same way. Again, if you have ever tasted your own tears as they run down to your mouth you'll know that they are rather salty and this, too, links us with the animals. Some animals cry rather a lot because it is a way of ridding the body of excess salt. Animals that spend most of their time in the sea, like marine turtles, are often particular 'cry babies' and weep for much of the time, most noticeably when they come ashore to lay their eggs in the sand. The reason for this lies in the fact that their 'tear apparatus' is different from ours and the crocodile's. In crocodile and man, surplus lachrymal fluid runs away from the eye into the passages inside the nose. That is why you may have to blow your nose after a good cry. Turtles have no such 'overflow system', so that all of their tears run down their cheeks. No wonder they look so miserable!

The green sea turtle, 'crying'.

ARE ELEPHANTS FRIGHTENED BY MICE ?

When you visit a zoo, it is likely that the elephants are among the animals you make a point of seeing first, because they are truly impressive and unique creatures. The largest land animals on earth, they weigh up to six tons and are so powerful that it is hard to imagine them ever being afraid of anything. In the wild, in fact, they have no enemies, apart from man, who still kills them for their ivory tusks. Even that so-called 'king of the beasts', the lion, will never attack a full-grown elephant. Where, then, does the old idea of elephants being frightened by tiny mice come from? Is it some some sort of joke or could it be based on faulty observation?

The answer is by no means easy to provide. It seems unlikely to come from *wild* elephants, because it is doubtful if they ever come into contact with mice in their natural habitat — and, even if they did, their reaction would be difficult to see, since trying to get near to wild elephants is a risky business!

If there *is* anything in the idea, then, it probably comes from captive or tame elephants, and here we have rather more to go on, because, apart from being kept in zoos, elephants have been used by man for one purpose or another for thousands of years. Usually gentle giants in captivity, elephants were employed for riding and traction in the Indus Valley of India as long ago as 2000 B.C., and there is a continuous history of elephant domestication since that time. Even today, Asiatic or Indian elephants (slightly smaller than their African cousins) are trained to do heavy work, like shifting timbers, in countries such as Burma and Sri Lanka.

Working Indian elephants in Thailand.

280BC: Pyrrhus, King of Epirus, riding his war elephant.

218BC: Hannibal and his elephants cross the Alps.

Both Asiatic and African elephants have also been used in war, for carrying supplies and men and to strike terror into the hearts of enemies who might not have seen these great beasts before. One of the most famous uses of elephants for this purpose was by the Carthaginian general, Hannibal, who attacked Rome with an army containing about fifty African elephants in 218 B.C.

Of course, to soldiers unused to meeting elephants in battle, these great beasts must have seemed strange and terrifying indeed. However, the advantage does not seem to have been always one-way, because there is evidence that elephants were much less steady under fire than horses, mules and other animals used for riding and baggage. They might have alarmed the enemy but they were probably equally terrified themselves! And who can blame them because the sheer stress of battle — the clash of arms, the cries of soldiers, flights of arrows, perhaps the smell of burning (animals hate fire) — would all have been highly alarming to the poor beasts and sufficient to set them off on a stampede. In fact, so unreliable were elephants in battle that they often proved more dangerous to their own side than to the opposition. After all, imagine the chaotic and demoralizing effect which might have been caused if one elephant felt it had had enough and decided to retreat through the following army!

India: Akbar, 16th Century Mogal Emperor, breaks a bridge with his elephants.

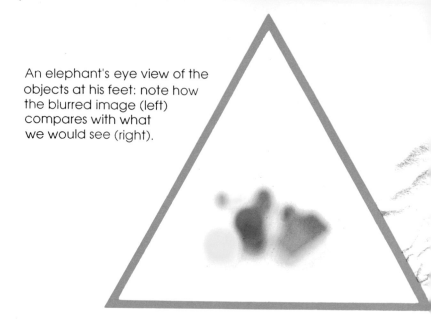

An elephant's eye view of the objects at his feet: note how the blurred image (left) compares with what we would see (right).

But where, you probably ask, do the mice come in? Well, the link is none too clear, but what we can say is that one reason for the elephants' excitability probably lies in the fact that they do not really know what is going on around their feet. Elephants can hear and smell very well, but their vision is much less good and basically designed for seeing what is just ahead of them. An elephant's idea of what is happening at ground level is less clear because its rather small eyes suffer from a sort of *astigmatism,* or blurring of the image, when it tries to see what action is taking place immediately beneath it.

Maybe this is what forms the basis of the idea that elephants fear mice, because it is quite possible that mice have got into zoo elephants' enclosures from time to time and prompted the bigger animals' violent reaction. An elephant would not be frightened of mice, as animals. It might not even recognize them. What it might do is object to the noise they made about its feet, as well as perhaps their smell, because it wouldn't know what caused either of these things!

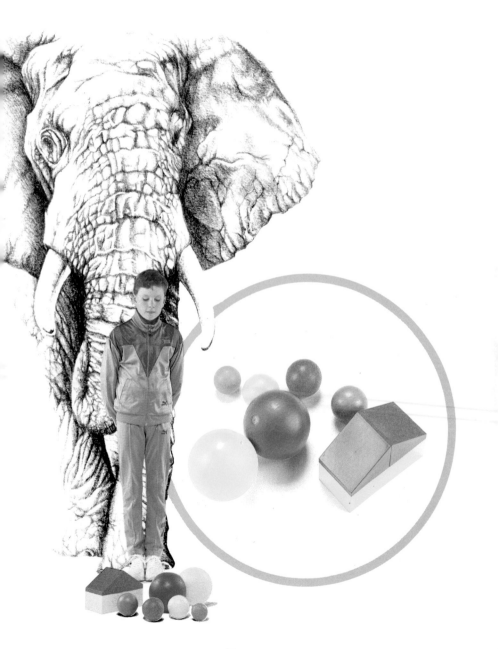

Some years ago, two American researchers went some way towards proving the point by deliberately releasing some rats and mice in an elephant's enclosure. Although some of the rodents were white and therefore easy to see, the elephants took not the slightest notice of them, even when they ran over their great feet. The only thing that did bother them, it seems, was the rustling noise the mice and rats made as they scampered in and out of the straw. This immediately set the elephants off trumpeting and rampaging. Just as we might be alarmed by strange unidentifiable noises heard at night, the elephants expressed their fear of what they could not see or understand. It is also possible that the rodents' rustling movements made the elephants think of the crackling outbreak of fire.

Indian elephants.

African elephant.

To sum up, then, it seems likely that the 'elephant and mice' belief came about because someone saw an elephant's reaction to a mouse's movements about its feet and drew quite the wrong conclusion. The tale may also have been kept going because there is something strangely attractive and amusing about the idea of big chaps being made to look silly or uncomfortable by little ones!

DOES THE OSTRICH BURY ITS HEAD IN THE SAND ?

Imagine you are lying in bed in a strange house. The light is out and you are just dropping off to sleep when you suddenly hear a strange noise coming from somewhere in the room. (To make it more spooky, let's say there's no bedside lamp and you'll have to get out of bed to switch the light on!) What do you do? Go and investigate or pull the duvet over your head and pretend there's nothing there?

Well, I can't put myself in your place, of course, but if you did try to ignore the situation you might well be described as having a 'head in the sand' attitude, because that's the way we refer to people who deliberately avoid the issue or don't have the courage to face up to reality. 'Ignore it and it will go away' might describe the basic idea.

Ostriches in the Kalahari.

Probably few people think of the ostrich when they use the expression today, yet that, it seems, is where it originally came from. Early naturalists believed that, in times of danger, this great flightless bird didn't always run away or try to defend itself but simply stayed where it was and literally buried its head in the sand or perhaps a bush, thinking that this somehow made it invisible to its enemies.

Yes, it does sound silly now, I agree, as well as a bit of an insult to the ostrich's intelligence, so how on earth did the idea arise in the first place? Ostriches are shy birds and very difficult to approach. Able to run at up to about sixty kilometres an hour, they certainly don't hang around to bury their heads in the sand, and if they did it would be surely easy to prove because the birds would not see us coming! Clearly, the idea must have been based on faulty observation to some extent, plus a good deal of vivid imagination and (perhaps) a sense of humour thrown in.

To solve the mystery, we need to look at how the ostrich lives and behaves in its natural habitat, which nowadays is mostly the arid scrubland of East Africa, although at one time its range extended over a much wider area of the continent. The largest bird on earth, the ostrich stands about 1.20 metres high at the shoulders, with another 1.20 metres or so making up its long, narrow, almost featherless neck. Males and females (cocks and hens) are roughly the same size but very differently coloured. Cocks have glossy black feathers on their rounded bodies and bottom of the neck, as well as brilliant white tail feathers, whereas females and immature birds are much duller, being mostly grey-brown.

For much of the time, ostriches go about in large herds of perhaps fifty or so birds. In the breeding season, however, group numbers tend to be smaller, a herd commonly consisting of one adult male and several hens, together with some immature birds. Each of the hens lays her eggs in a communal nest, and one of the hens incubates the eggs, although 'incubation' mainly consists of protecting the eggs from the fierce

Male ostrich distracts predators from his young.

African sun. The hen does this both with her body and by spreading her short wings over them.

This sort of arrangement works well because it means that while the one hen looks after the eggs, the male and other birds can keep a sharp look-out for enemies, between nibbling food, such as coarse desert plants, lizards and insects. Never roaming far from the nest (which is no more than a hollow in the ground), they have sharp eyesight and are forever twisting and turning their long necks to watch for danger. If enemies do threaten — a pack of wild dogs or hyenas, perhaps — the standing birds may do a variety of things. They may run away for a short distance or perform a sort of broken-wing, distraction display, designed to draw the predators away from the eggs or young — running hither and thither, shaking and lowering their short wings or kicking up great clouds of dust with their large, strongly-toed feet, with which they can also deliver a powerful kick.

Of course, even the brooding female has to abandon the eggs in the end, when she becomes physically threatened, but she only leaves them at the last moment. She may not even be seen because when sitting on the eggs she takes up a position with her head lowered to the ground in front of her, so as to make herself look less conspicuous. From a distance, she looks very like a mere hummock in the sand, and it is probably partly this that gave rise to the 'head in the sand' idea, particularly since ostriches rarely let human observers get closer than about a hundred yards away.

Far from being stupid, as the old saying suggests, ostriches are really rather clever in the way they protect their eggs and young. As we have seen, only the hens brood the eggs during the day, because their dull plumage makes them difficult to spot. The cock also takes his turn with nest duties, but he does so only at night, when his contrasting black and white plumage is less noticeable and might even enable him to be mistaken for a shadowed bush!

There are other aspects of ostrich behaviour which may have given rise to the head-in-the-sand notion. One lies in the fact that ostriches commonly hold their heads close to the ground to pick up the vibrations of approaching enemies. Even their sleeping position might have added to the impression, because the birds then sit on their haunches with their heads thrust out in front of them and resting on the ground. Of course, ostriches are

unlikely to be 'caught napping' like this because there are always some of the herd on watch. Sometimes, too, ostriches deliberately seek the company of antelope and zebra, moving about with them and using them as extra observers of approaching danger.

Ostriches, surrounded by wildebeast and zebras, watch out for danger.

Ostriches perform this display before settling their chicks in a safe place.

The 'head-in-the-sand' myth is not the only story to make the ostrich seem to be a foolish bird. Another is the idea that the birds will eat almost anything. You may have seen cartoons and comic strips showing ostriches swallowing all manner of strange objects, including bottles, which are often illustrated as being stuck halfway down their long necks. It is doubtful if ostriches ever go quite so far as that, although they are certainly known to gobble up a variety of strange and quite inedible items, at least partly because they have only a poorly developed sense of taste. In any case, the action has little to do with feeding, as such. It is simply a method the birds use to help their digestion. Mostly, they swallow stones, grit and sand, because these items assist the stomach to break down the tough foods they eat, but they have also been known to gulp down lumps of iron and even, in zoos and on ostrich farms, to snatch the buttons off people's coats!

Bright, glittering objects seem to have a particular fascination for the ostrich. In fact, the writer H. G. Wells made use of this theme in a short story, which tells of an ostrich which was supposed to have swallowed a valuable diamond. A number of other, much smaller birds, such as jackdaws and magpies, have a similar liking for bright things which they often steal and take back to their nests. No one really knows why.

DOES THE CAMEL
STORE WATER
IN ITS
HUMP ?

I don't suppose you have ever been stranded in the desert, but there must have been times when you were very thirsty, perhaps after a long hike which took you far from a tap or shop. You might even have wished, in situations such as these, that you were like a camel and carried your own built-in water-store — except that you could do without the permanent hump!

Unfortunately, this traditional image we have of the 'ship of the desert' is far from accurate. Camels *are* very much better adapted than we are for surviving for long periods without water in very hot, dry climates, but neither the one-humped Arabian nor the two-humped Bactrian or Syrian camel actually stores water in its humps. The camels' humps do have an important part to play in their lives, but not quite in the way the old idea has it.

Dromedary or Arabian camel.

Bactrian or Syrian camel.

To appreciate how the 'water-hump' belief came about requires a closer look at the camel's survival technique in general, and this is best done with the Arabian camel. Both kinds can be seen in zoos, of course, but it is mostly the Arabian camel (sometimes called the dromedary) that is the most familiar, being used for riding and carrying supplies over a wide area of North Africa and the Middle East. Camels are particularly useful in areas like these, where daytime temperatures commonly soar above 100°F (38°C), rains are few and far between, and oases widely separated, because they need much less care and attention than other domesticated animals, such as asses and horses. They are not deliberately neglected by their human masters, of course, but they can, if necessary, go for weeks without food or water, subsisting at most on sparse desert plants. They certainly do not suffer from the effects of extreme thirst in the way that we do in similar circumstances. If we were subjected to extreme heat and were unable to

Camels before the Pyramids at Giza, Egypt.

drink for two or three days we would almost certainly die from dehydration, or water loss.

There are a number of reasons why camels are able to stand the heat and dryness so well. One lies in the fact that their bodies do not heat up so rapidly as ours do, so that they sweat much less. Sweating, as I am sure you know, is the body's way of cooling us down when we become overheated, but of course it has a boomerang effect in making us lose precious water. The more we sweat to keep cool, the thirstier we become. Sweating works well enough for a time but the water lost in this way must eventually be replaced if we are to survive.

Camels not only sweat very much less than we do but the effects of their water-loss are much less drastic than they are with us. In humans, excessive sweating

57

eventually involves water being removed from the blood, as well as from the general body tissues. This has the effect of making our blood thicker and more difficult for the heart to pump around the body. This, in turn, places a great strain on the heart and causes eventual heart-failure.

By contrast, the camel loses hardly any water from its blood during times when it cannot drink, so that there is much less strain on the heart. It does lose water from its body tissues or flesh, and actually shrinks to some extent, but that doesn't bother it to any great degree. In addition to all this, the camel's urine is more highly concentrated during times of drought and lost in much smaller quantities, while its droppings are virtually dry.

Another point that makes camels so much superior to us in the water-conservation stakes lies in their ability to make up for lost time when they *are* able to drink. Men literally almost dying of thirst are always given only small drinks at first, because to take in a large amount of water at once would be almost as bad as having none at all. Uncontrolled drinking directly after two or three days of thirst can have disastrous effects, in diluting the blood too rapidly. Indeed, in cases like this, it is possible for a human being to become, quite literally, 'drunk on water' or, worse, die from water intoxication. A camel has no such problems. It can take in as much as 100-150 litres at one go and in a very few minutes, without turning a hair. By so doing, it becomes almost magically transformed from a thin, starved-looking creature into a fat, healthy-looking animal, fit for anything. This is because the water goes straight into its tissues and not its blood.

Actually, this is where the camel's humps come in. The belief that it stored water in them is understandable because when the camel is well-fed and watered the humps are solid and firm, whereas in times of water scarcity they become smaller, soft and flabby. It really does seem as if the camel has lived off its hump, during the time it was parched. In a sense it did, too, except that the humps contain fat, not water, this being broken down and used as a reserve energy store when the camel cannot eat. Even the hump's position on the camel's back makes sense because if the fat were more evenly spread over its body it would act like a blanket and make the animal overheated. Perched on top of the animal, protected from the fierce sun by a thick matt of tough hair, it is out of the way and much less trouble!

THE CAMEL'S HABITAT

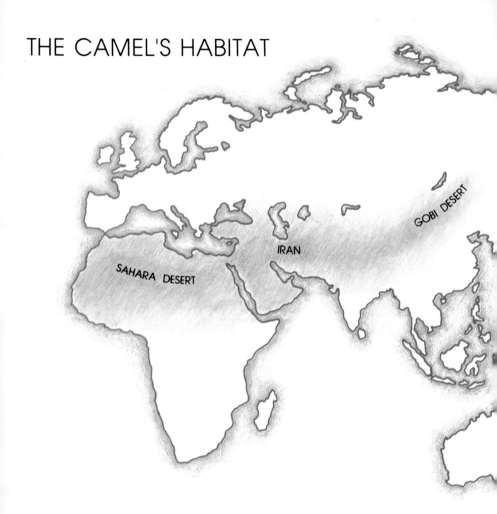

If you look at both kinds of camel in a zoo, you will note that the Bactrian camel displays slight differences from its Arabian cousin, apart from the extra hump. One is its shorter legs, another, its heavier, shaggier coat. These features are linked to the Bactrian's habitat, which is nowadays mostly Central Asia, especially the Gobi Desert, where it is much colder and the Bactrian camel's thicker coat stands it in good stead.

At one time, Bactrian camels lived and were domesticated over a wide area of the Middle East and Asia. Indeed, its name comes from Bactria, an ancient province of Persia, the modern Iran. However, they were long ago superseded by the Arabian, which is better adapted to living and working in very dry conditions. Some Bactrian camels are used by Central Asian tribesmen for riding and baggage-carrying but

A camel train in Iran.

others still live wild. They are, in fact, the only wild camels left because the one-humped Arabian now exists only as a domesticated animal.

The interesting thing is that the two may really be merely varieties of one species because they readily interbreed. When such crosses occur, the young often have two humps, which suggests that the original camel ancestor was closer to the Bactrian.

Camels have been good servants to man for many centuries but, in some ways, they are still only semi-domesticated. Indeed, they have a certain reputation for being bad-tempered, which could be where we gained the expression 'to have the hump'! Camels have also given us another figure of speech, which is linked to their own very firm ideas of how hard they should be made to work. A camel will uncomplainingly carry burdens of up to 180 kilograms but many travellers have recorded how, if a camel felt it was being overburdened or 'put upon' by even the smallest amount, it refused to get up until its load was lightened. Translated into popular, everyday terms, this became 'the straw that broke the camel's back' or, more commonly, the 'last straw'. In other words, it is the final disappointment or set-back, which might have been small in itself but followed a long line of disasters, making us finally lose patience and temper and give up — like the camel.

This book is to be returned on or before
the last date stamped below.

LIBREX

WOOTTON.   296627